$15.95

D1282856

BOOKWORMS

Safe Kids
Fire Safety

Niños seguros
Seguridad en caso de incendio

Dana Meachen Rau

Marshall Cavendish
Benchmark
New York

Never play with matches.

One small match can start a big fire.

Nunca juegues con fósforos.

Un pequeño fósforo puede iniciar un gran incendio.

Do not get too close to fire.

Even candles can burn you.

———◆———

No te acerques demasiado al fuego.

Hasta las velas pueden quemarte.

Watch out for flames on the stove.

Your clothes can catch on fire.

Ten cuidado con las llamas de la estufa.

Tu ropa puede prenderse fuego.

Do not sit too close to a *fireplace*.

Sparks can come out and burn you.

No te sientes muy cerca de una *chimenea*.

Las chispas pueden saltar y quemarte.

Your house needs to have *smoke alarms*.

Beep! Beep! They warn you of a fire.

Tu casa debe tener *alarmas de humo*.

¡Pip! ¡Pip! Te advierten si hay un incendio.

If you hear them beep, leave the house.

A fire truck will hurry to help you.

Si las oyes sonar, sal de la casa.

Un camión de bomberos llegará rápidamente para ayudarte.

Practice a fire plan with your family.

You need two safe ways to get out.

———————❖———————

Practica un plan contra incendios con tu familia.

Necesitas dos salidas seguras.

Do not hide.

Firefighters need to find you.

No te escondas.

Los bomberos tienen que encontrarte.

Never open a hot door.

Feel your door first to see if it is hot.

———◆———

Nunca abras una puerta caliente.

Primero toca la puerta para ver si está caliente.

Smoke may fill the room.

Crawl out on the floor below the smoke.

El humo puede llenar la habitación.

Sal arrastrándote sobre el suelo,
debajo del humo.

Your clothes could catch fire.

Stop, drop, and roll to put it out.

Tu ropa podría prenderse fuego.

Detente, échate al suelo y da vueltas para apagarlo.

Have a safe place to meet your family outside.

Never go back into a fire.

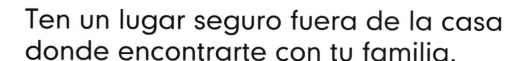

Ten un lugar seguro fuera de la casa donde encontrarte con tu familia.

Nunca vuelvas al incendio.

Be a safe kid with fire.

Sé un niño seguro con el fuego.

Be Safe
Estar seguro

candle
vela

fire truck
camión de bomberos

fireplace
chimenea

match
fósforo

smoke
humo

smoke alarm
alarma de humo

stop, drop, and roll
detente, échate al suelo y da vueltas

stove
estufa

Challenge Words

fireplace A safe place to hold a fire that is built in a wall at the base of a chimney.

smoke alarm A machine that beeps loudly to show there is smoke from a fire.

Palabras avanzadas

alarma de humo Aparato que suena fuerte para indicar que hay humo de un incendio.

chimenea Lugar seguro para encender el fuego que se construye en una pared en la base de un conducto.

Index

Page numbers in **boldface**
  are illustrations.

beeping, 10, 12, 29
burn, 4, 8

candle, 4, **5**, **27**, **28**
closeness, 4, 8
clothes, 6, 22
crawling, 20, **21**

fire plan, 14, **15**
fire truck, 12, **13**, **28**
firefighters, 16, **17**
fireplace, 8, **9**, **28**, 29
flames, 5, 6, **7**, **9**, **27**, **28**

hiding, **16**
hot door, 18, **19**

match, 2, 3, **28**
meeting place, 24, **25**

smoke, **11**, 20, **21**, **28**, 29
smoke alarm, 10, **11**, **28**, 29
sparks, 8
stop, drop, and roll, 22, **23**, **29**
stove, 6, **7**, **29**

warning, 10

Índice

Las páginas indicadas con números en
  negrita tienen ilustraciones.

acercarse, 4, 8
advertir, 10
alarma de humo, 10, **11**, **28**, 29
arrastrarse, 20, **21**

bomberos, 16, **17**

camión de bomberos, 12, **13**, **28**
chimenea, 8, **9**, **28**, 29
chispas, 8

detente, échate al suelo y da vueltas, 22,
  23, **29**

esconderse, **16**
estufa, 6, **7**, **29**

fósforo, 2, 3, **28**

humo, **11**, 20, **21**, **28**, 29

llamas, 5, 6, **7**, **9**, **27**, **28**
lugar donde encontrarse, 24, **25**

plan contra incendios, 14, **15**
puerta caliente, 18, **19**

quemar, 4, 8

ropa, 6, 22

sonar, 10, 12, 29

vela, 4, **5**, **27**, **28**

About the Author

Dana Meachen Rau is the author of many other titles in the Bookworms series, as well as other nonfiction and early reader books. She lives in Burlington, Connecticut, with her husband and two children.

Sobre la autora

Dana Meachen Rau es la autora de muchos libros de la serie Bookworms y de otros libros de no ficción y de lectura para principiantes. Vive en Burlington, Connecticut, con su esposo y sus dos hijos.

With thanks to the Reading Consultants:

Nanci Vargus, Ed.D., is an Assistant Professor of Elementary Education at the University of Indianapolis.

Beth Walker Gambro is an Adjunct Professor at the University of Saint Francis in Joliet, Illinois.

Agradecemos a las asesoras de lectura:

Nanci Vargus, doctora en Educación, es profesora auxiliar de Educación Primaria en la Universidad de Indianápolis.

Beth Walker Gambro es profesora adjunta en la Universidad de Saint Francis en Joliet, Illinois.

Marshall Cavendish Benchmark
99 White Plains Road
Tarrytown, New York 10591
www.marshallcavendish.us

Text copyright © 2010 by Marshall Cavendish Corporation

Library of Congress Cataloging-in-Publication Data

Rau, Dana Meachen, 1971–
[Fire safety. Spanish & English]
Fire safety = Seguridad en caso de incendio / Dana Meachen Rau.
p. cm. — (Bookworms. Safe kids = Niños seguros)
Includes bibliographical references and index.
Parallel text in English and Spanish; translated from the English.
ISBN 978-0-7614-4784-9 (bilingual ed.) — ISBN 978-0-7614-4091-8 (English ed.)
1. Fire prevention—Juvenile literature. 2. Fires—Safety measures—Juvenile literature.
I. Title. II. Title: Seguridad en caso de incendio.
TH9148.R4418 2009
628.9'2—dc22
2009016369

Editor: Christina Gardeski
Publisher: Michelle Bisson
Designer: Virginia Pope
Art Director: Anahid Hamparian

Spanish Translation and Text Composition by Victory Productions, Inc.
www.victoryprd.com

Photo Research by Anne Burns Images

Cover Photo by *Photo Edit*/Myrleen Pearson

The photographs in this book are used with permission and through the courtesy of:
Getty Images: pp. 1, 11, 28BR Stephen Marks; p. 27 China Tourism Press.
Corbis: pp. 3, 28BL Chris Collins; pp. 9, 28TR Benelux/zefa; p. 25 James Leynse.
SuperStock: pp. 5, 28TL Photononstop; pp. 7, 29R Prisma; pp. 13, 19, 28TC age fotostock;
p. 17 SuperStock. *Photo Edit*: p. 15 Michael Newman; pp. 21, 28 Kayte Deioma;
pp. 23, 29L Richard Hutchings.

Printed in Malaysia
1 3 5 6 4 2

DATE DUE